Blend Hunt

Set 2

Written by Kassi Gilmour   Illustrated by Joan Gilmour

Practise the sounds

m s t a p i f c r
o d h e n g k ck

The Blend Hunt books are designed to help children practise blending new sounds within each set. Once each word is successfully blended, children search for the item that matches the words they have read on each page.

Practise tricky words

I my the is a
he she to do

Blend Hunt

Set 2

Written by Kassi Gilmour   Illustrated by Joan Gilmour

hen egg

pig pen

rock crack

ram sip

hot pot

| s | a | ck | | s | c | r | a | p |

Nan hat

man snip

Nan

Written by Kassi Gilmour   Illustrated by Joan Gilmour

Practise the sounds

m s t a p i f c r
o d h e n g k ck

Practise blending sounds

Dad   Nan   drops
off   pets   eggs
pink   pest   tops

Practise tricky words

I my the is a
he she to too do

Nan

Set 2

Written by Kassi Gilmour   Illustrated by Joan Gilmour

Dad drops Sam off at Nan's.

Nan's is rad. She has pets.

Nan has a pink pig in the pig pen.

She has a ram. It sips at the dam.

Nan has hens too. She can get eggs from the hens.

Nan has a rat. It is a pest!

Tam can get the rat. Tam is Nan's cat.

Mack is Nan's dog, and he is tops.

Questions:

1. How does Sam get to Nan's house?
2. What pets does Nan have?
3. Which one does Sam like best? How do you know?
4. What pet would you like and why?

Hens

Written by Kassi Gilmour   Illustrated by Joan Gilmour

Practise the sounds

m s t a p i f c r
o d h e n g k ck

Practise blending sounds

S a m   h e n   e gg

n o t   p e ck   s p o t

t r i p   c r a ck

Practise tricky words

I my the is a
he she to do

Hens

Set 2

Written by Kassi Gilmour   Illustrated by Joan Gilmour

Sam is at the hens.

He can spot the eggs.

A mess on the rocks.

Questions:

1. Where is Sam?
2. What does Sam do?
3. Why might the hen peck?
4. Have you seen a chicken's nesting box?

Pig

Written by Kassi Gilmour   Illustrated by Joan Gilmour

Practise the sounds

m s t a p i f c r
o d h e n g k ck

Practise blending sounds

Sam pig get

pen off pink

scrap packs

Practise tricky words

I my the is a
he she to do

Pig

Set 2

Written by Kassi Gilmour   Illustrated by Joan Gilmour

Sam gets the scraps.

He packs the scraps in a sack.

Off to the pig pen.

The pig is in the pen.

She is pink.

He drops the scraps in the pen.

The pig can get the scraps.

Sam fed the pig.

Questions:

1. What does Sam do?
2. Why is he packing a bag?
3. Describe the pig?
4. Have you seen a pig? If so, what was it doing?

Ram

Written by Kassi Gilmour   Illustrated by Joan Gilmour

Practise the sounds

m s t a p i f c r
o d h e n g k ck

Practise blending sounds

Sam ram dam
hot gets snip
ramp off toss

Practise tricky words

I my the is a
he she to too do

Ram

Set 2

Written by Kassi Gilmour   Illustrated by Joan Gilmour

The ram is at the dam.

It is too hot. Sip, sip, sip.

Sam gets the ram at the dam.

He drags him off to get a trim.

Snip, snip, snip.

Toss the ram on the ramp.

He ran to the dam.

The ram is not hot.

Questions:

1. Where is the ram?
2. Why is he at the dam?
3. How will being sheared help?
4. What do you think they will do with the wool?

Snack

Written by Kassi Gilmour Illustrated by Joan Gilmour

Practise the sounds

m s t a p i f c r
o d h e n g k ck

Practise blending sounds

Sam   Nan   dip

pot   eggs   nags

snack   crack

Practise tricky words

I my the is a
he she to do

Snack

Set 2

Written by Kassi Gilmour   Illustrated by Joan Gilmour

Sam is at Nan's.

He nags Nan to get a snack.

Nan gets the eggs.

The pot is hot.

She drops the eggs in the pot.

Crack the egg.

Sam dips in the egg.

Dip, dip, dip.

It is hot!

Nan fed Sam his eggs.

Questions:

1. Where is Sam?
2. What does he want?
3. Why does Nan have to feed him?
4. How do you like your eggs?